T0198493

THE
Holy Spirit:
AN UNTAPPED RESERVOIR

THE
Holy Spirit:
An Untapped Reservoir

FLOYD VEAL JR.

authorHOUSE®

AuthorHouse™
1663 Liberty Drive
Bloomington, IN 47403
www.authorhouse.com
Phone: 1-800-839-8640

© 2013 by Floyd Veal Jr. All rights reserved.

No part of this book may be reproduced, stored in a retrieval system, or transmitted by any means without the written permission of the author.

Published by AuthorHouse   03/22/2013

ISBN: 978-1-4817-2998-7 (sc)
ISBN: 978-1-4817-2997-0 (e)

Library of Congress Control Number: 2013904901

Any people depicted in stock imagery provided by Thinkstock are models, and such images are being used for illustrative purposes only.
Certain stock imagery © Thinkstock.

This book is printed on acid-free paper.

Because of the dynamic nature of the Internet, any web addresses or links contained in this book may have changed since publication and may no longer be valid. The views expressed in this work are solely those of the author and do not necessarily reflect the views of the publisher, and the publisher hereby disclaims any responsibility for them.

DEDICATION

To God the Father for so loving this world that he gave his only begotten son and that who so ever believes in him shall not but have everlasting life.

To Jesus for his obedience unto death that we may life and have it more abundately.

To the Holy Spirit for dwelling with me, leading me into al truth and giving me this revelation to the rest of the world.

TABLE OF CONTENTS

TABLE OF CONTENTS

INTRODUCTION

———— ∞ ————

Holy, Holy, Holy Spirit. My Comforter, my Counselor, my Sustainer. I love Him and I am thankful that He has given me the privilege and honor to write this book about Him. He revealed Himself to me as a "Reservoir". The definition of a reservoir is a place where water is collected and stored for use. It can also be defined as a great supply of something. Comparatively, the Holy Spirit (Who is a Person) contains an everlasting supply of living water. John 7:37-39 reads that:

> On the last day, that great day of the feast, Jesus stood and cried out, saying, "If anyone thirsts, let him come to Me and drink. He who believes in me, as the scripture has said, out of his heart will flow rivers of living water." But this He spoke concerning the Spirit, whom those

> *believing in Him would receive; for the Holy Spirit was not yet given, because Jesus was not yet glorified.*

Water is one of the many emblems or symbols of the Holy Spirit. 1 John 5:7-8 says: *For there are three that bear witness in heaven: The Father, The Word, and the Holy Spirit; and these agree as one. And these three are one. And there are three that bear witness on earth: the Spirit, the water, and the blood; and these agree as one.* And like water He quenches our thirst whether it be physically, mentally, emotionally, or spiritually. Isaiah 44:3 says: *For I will pour water out on him who is thirsty, And floods on the dry ground; I will pour My Spirit on your descendants, And My blessing on your offspring.* In John 4:13-14: *Jesus answered and said to her, "Whoever drinks of the water that I shall give him will never thirst. But the water that I shall give him will become in him a fountain of water springing up into everlasting life."* Isaiah 55:1: *"Ho! Everyone who thirsts, Come to the waters; Yes, come and buy and eat. Yes, come, buy wine and milk without money and without price.* Revelations 22:17 says: *And the Spirit and the bride say, "Come!" And let him who hears say, "Come!" And let him who thirsts come. Whoever desires, let him take the water of life freely. Now this living water can and will cleanse us of unrighteousness and filthiness.* Ezekiel 36:25: *"Then I will sprinkle clean water on you, and you shall be clean; I will cleanse you from all your filthiness and from all your idols.*

The Holy Spirit is present with everyone who has received the baptism of the Holy Spirit, but we have not harnessed His full potential nor ours. Jesus came as a Lamb offering to die for man for his redemption, but also that the Holy Spirit could continue the work that Jesus started. This impartation which was received on Pentecost blessed everyone who was present to speak with new tongues of fire. He empowered them with boldness to proclaim to Gospel of Jesus Christ with signs and wonders following. In John14:12, Jesus says: "*Most assuredly, I say to you, he who believes in Me, the works that I do he will do also; and greater works than these he will do, because I go to My father.* Most Christians do not really know the Holy Spirit and limit Him just to praying in tongues and have not found the full revelation of Whom He really is. He connects with us and allows us to have fellowship with Him, Jesus and The Father. Ephesians 2:18 says: *For through Him we both have access by one Spirit to the Father.* Jesus 16:14-15 says: *He will glorify me, for He will take of what is Mine and declare it to you. All things that the Father has are mine. Therefore I said that He will take of Mine and declare it to you. I sometimes envy the disciples who were able to talk and walk with Jesus, but we also have access to him by the Holy Spirit.* Rom. 8:9-11 says: But you are not in the flesh but in the Spirit, if indeed the Spirit of God dwells in you. Now if anyone does not have the Spirit of Christ, he is not His. And if Christ is in you, the body is dead because of sin, but the Spirit is life because of righteousness. But if the Spirit of him who raised Jesus from the dead dwells in you, He who raised Christ from the dead will also give life to your mortal bodies through His Spirit who dwells in you. So having the Holy Spirit is the same as having Jesus living in you. Now it was noted earlier that the Holy Spirit is a reservoir. He feels that He is untapped and that is why I am writing about Him. In this book I am going to further discuss the seven spirits that dwell within the Holy Spirit and how we are to tap into this ever flowing river of the Third Person of the eternal God-Head.

CHAPTER 1

⸺⚬⚭⚬⸺

The Spirit of the Lord: Supernatural
Transformation

Now the first time I read this scripture, Isaiah 11:2, I was intrigued. The verse says The Spirit of the Lord shall rest upon Him, The Spirit of wisdom and understanding, The Spirit of Counsel and Might, The Spirit of knowledge and of the fear of the Lord.

When I first read it, I only saw six spirits and I remembered my pastor taught that there were seven spirits, so I was little confused. I read it again and I found that I had overlooked the first spirit: The Spirit of the Lord. This Spirit contains the essential power and presence of God. It also contains life, and all of the other six derive from and flow from this Spirit. The definition of "Lord" is—one with authority over others. It is also defined as a person who exercises authority from property rights; an owner of land or houses.

As God made Adam in His image and His likeness ad breathed into his nostrils the breath of life, He has given man authority over everything on the earth except other men. He was naked, but the shekinah glory covered him, which is symbolic of the Holy Spirit. The Hebrew and Greek words translated "spirit" are *ruach* and *pneuma*, both meaning literally "wind" or "breath." That is why Adam was born as an adult and was intelligent enough to name every living creature. When God breathed upon him, He literally breathed into his spirit with the Holy Spirit. Psalm 24:1 says: *The earth is lords and all its fullness, The world and those who dwell therein.* This scripture is telling us that the earth and everything that was created and to be created was for His pleasure and He owns it all. That is where we get the word landlord from; someone who owns and exercises authority over the land.

The Spirit of the Lord contains transforming, creative power. Genesis 1:1-3 says: *In the beginning God created the heavens and earth. The earth was without form and void; and darkness was on the face of the deep. And the Spirit of God was hovering over the face of the waters.* Now as the rest of the first chapter of Genesis continues, we see that every word that God spoke was given life by the Holy Spirit.

It was also the Holy Spirit that transformed the Word of God into Mary and as a result, Jesus Christ was born. Luke 1:30-32 says: *Then the angel said to her, "Do not be afraid, Mary, for you have found favor with God. "And behold, you will conceive in you womb and bring forth a Son, and shall call his name Jesus.* 34-35: *Then Mary said to the angel, "How can this be, since I do not know a man?" And the angel answered and said to her, "The Holy Spirit will come upon you, and the power of the Highest will overshadow you; therefore, also, that Holy One who is born will be called the Son of God.*

John 1:14 states: *And the word became flesh and dwelt among us and we beheld His glory as of the only begotten of the Father, full of grace and truth.* Revelation 19:13 states: *He was clothed with a robe dipped in blood, and His name is called the Word of God.* After Jesus was baptized by John the Baptist, the Holy Spirit came upon Him to minister unto the people. Matthew 3:16 says: *When he had been baptized, Jesus came up immediately from the water: and behold, the heavens were opened to Him, and He saw the Spirit of God descending like a dove and alighting upon him.* Jesus was empowered by this Holy Spirit with miracle, wonder—working power. He was given knowledge and authority for His ministry. That is why it was so important that His disciples would receive the Holy Spirit so that they could operate as he did. At that time He was the only one that had the Holy Spirit. In John 14:12, He told them: *Most assuredly, I say to you, he who believes in Me, the works that I do he will do also; and greater works*

3

than these he will do, because I go to My father. Jesus gave them some of the Holy Spirit, but it was not the complete endowment. It was only a sustainer until the day of Pentecost. John 20:21-22 states: *So Jesus said to them again, "Peace to you! As the Father has sent Me, I also send you." And when He had said this, He breathed on them and said to them, "Receive the Holy Spirit.* Now after the day of Pentecost, the disciples went out and preached, boldy proclaiming the name of Jesus Christ and the Holy Spirit working with signs and wonders. Peter's first sermon added 3,000 souls to the kingdom of God. Acts 2:37-43 says:

> Now when they heard this, they were cut to the heart, and said to Peter and the rest of the apostles, "Men and brethren, what shall we do?" Then Peter said to them, "Repent and let every one of you be baptized in the name of Jesus Christ for the remission sins; and you shall receive the gift of the Holy Spirit. "For the promise is to you and to your children, and to all who are afar off, as many as the Lord our God will call." And with many other words he testified and exhorted them, saying, "Be saved from this perverse generation." Then those who gladly received his word were baptized; and that day about three thousand souls were added to them. And they continued steadfastly in the apostles' doctrine and fellowship, in the breaking of bread, and in prayers. Then fear came

upon every soul, and many wonders and signs were done through the apostles.

Paul said it best in 2 Corinthians 3:17-18: *Now the Lord is the Spirit; and where the Spirit of the Lord is, there is liberty. But we all, with unveiled face, beholding as in a mirror the glory of the Lord, are being transformed into the same image from glory to glory, just as by the Spirit of the Lord.* Now in the transformation you see liberty or freedom from the law and sin, but also a metamorphosis from child to Son of God. Romans 8:15-17 states: *For you did not receive the spirit of bondage again to fear, but you have received the spirit of adoption by whom we cry out, "Abba, Father." The Spirit Himself bears witness with our spirit that we are children of God. And if children, then heirs—heirs with God and joint heirs with Christ . . .* In John 3:5-6 Jesus answered: *"Most assuredly, I say to you, unless one is born of water and the Spirit, he cannot enter the kingdom of God. That which is born of flesh is flesh, and that which born of the Spirit is Spirit.*

2 Corinthians 3:3 *Clearly you are an epistle of Christ, ministered by us, written not with ink but by the Spirit of the living God, not on tablets of stone but on tablets of flesh, that is of the heart.* Titus 3:4-7 states: *But when the kindness and the love of God our Savior toward man appeared, not by works of righteousness which we have done, but according to His mercy He saved us, through the washing of regeneration and renewing of the Holy Spirit, whom he poured out on us abundantly through Jesus Christ*

our Savior, that having been justified by His grace we should become heirs according to the hope of eternal life.

1 Corinthians 12:13 *For by one Spirit we were all baptized into one body-whether Jews or Greeks, whether slaves or free—and have all been made to drink into one Spirit.*

A PERSONAL ENCOUNTER

One night, I was leaving prayer service at my church and an interesting thing happened. My spirit was charged and I was headed home to act on the word that I had received. I saw in the word how Jesus commanded things and whatever he spoke they had to obey. Now, I came home to my mother's house and asked her, "Is there anything in the house that is broken?" She asked me, "Why?" I said, "Because I want to speak to it and command it to work in Jesus' name." So she said, "Your father has to go to work, but the truck won't start. Instead going outside to lay hands on the truck, I stayed in the house and commanded it to work in Jesus' name. Now at this time I felt the presence of God all over me, yet I didn't think to go and start the car immediately. However, my brother came in a moment later running, screaming and praising God. I admit I got a little bit scared, but I asked him what had happened. What I did not know is that the Lord had told my brother to try and start the truck and when he did, Oh glory, the truck started right up! Needless to say, we praised

God with all of our might, but God was not finished yet. After we had calmed down somewhat, my mother asked me to pray for her and my brother also asked for prayer, because God was moving by His Spirit and answering all of our prayers.

My mother was so excited about all that God was doing that when my aunt called she told her about everything that was going on. My aunt, who was suffering from severe diarrhea, told my mother to have me pray for her. I immediately spoke to the condition and commanded that she be healed. I had to work a third shift that night and did not get home until the next day. When I came home my mother gave me the victory report about my aunt. She testified that when she got off the phone that the diarrhea immediately left her.

CHAPTER 2

The Spirit of Wisdom The Principal Thing

Wisdom is the principal thing and God wants you to have His wisdom. Proverbs 4:7: *Wisdom is the principal thing; therefore get wisdom.* This wisdom is not speaking of man's wisdom, but of the wisdom of God. 1 Corinthians 3:18-20 states: *Let no one deceive himself. If anyone among you seems to be wise in this age, let him become a fool that he may become wise. For the wisdom of this world is foolishness with God. For it is written, "He catches the wise in their own craftiness"; and again, "The Lord knows the thoughts of the wise, that they are futile."* Ephesians 1:17 adds *that the God of our Lord Jesus Christ, the Father of Glory, may give to you the spirit of wisdom and revelation in the knowledge of Him.* The Spirit of wisdom is the Spirit producing wisdom, or making one wise. Wisdom demonstrates the best means to secure the best ends. Romans 11:33 states: *Oh the depths of the riches both of the wisdom and knowledge of God! How unsearchable are His judgments and His ways past finding out!* This kind of spiritual wisdom produces happiness. Proverbs 3:13 says: *Happy is the man who finds wisdom.* Wisdom produces prosperity, but is greater than that fruit in itself. Proverbs 3:14-15 states: *For her proceeds are better than the profits of silver, And her gain than fine gold. She is more precious than rubies, And all the things you may desire cannot compare with her.* Proverbs 16:16: *How much better to get wisdom than gold!* The book of Job's take on Wisdom in Chapter 28:12-19 is:

> "But where can wisdom be found? And where is the place of understanding? Man does not its value, Nor is it found in the land of the living. The deep says, 'It is not in me'; And the sea says, 'It is not with me.' It cannot be purchased for gold, Nor can silver be weighed for its price. It cannot be valued in the gold of Ophir, in precious onyx or sapphire. Neither gold nor crystal can equal it, Nor can be exchanged for jewelry of fine gold. No mention shall be made of coral or quartz, For the price of wisdom is above rubies. The topaz of Ethiopia cannot equal it, Nor can it be valued in pure gold.

Wisdom also produces long life, peace, riches and honor. Proverbs 3:7-8 says: *Do not be wise in your own eyes; Fear the Lord and depart from evil. It will be health to your flesh, and strength to your bones.* Deuteronomy 4:5-6 instructs:

> "Surely I have taught you statutes and judgments, just as the Lord my God commanded me, that you should act according to them in the land which you go to possess. Therefore be careful to observe them; for this is your wisdom and your understanding in the sight of the peoples who will hear all these statutes, and say, "Surely this great nation is a wise and understanding people.""

Job came to know of God's wisdom in the time of his storm. Job 12: 7-13 says:

> But now ask the beasts, and they will teach you; And the birds of the air, and they will tell you; Or speak to the earth, and it will teach you; and the fish of the sea will explain to you. Who among all these does not know that the hand of the Lord has done this, in Whose hand is the life of every living thing, and the breath of all mankind? Does not the ear test words and the mouth taste its food? Wisdom is with the aged men, and with length of days, understanding. With Him are wisdom and strength, He has counsel and understanding.

This wisdom was personified by King Solomon when he first became king. He was a young king and did not have any experience and knowledge of being a king over God's people. He prayed and God gave him wisdom. 1 Kings 3:4-9 says:

> Now the king went to Gibeon to sacrifice there, for that was the great high place: Solomon offered a thousand burnt offerings on that altar. At Gibeon the Lord appeared to Solomon in a dream by night; and God said, "Ask! What shall I give you?" And Solomon said: "You have shown great mercy to Your servant David my father, because he walked before You in truth, in righteousness, and in uprightness of heart with You; You have continued this great kindness for him, and You have given him a son to sit on his throne, as it is this day. "Now, O Lord my God, You have made your king instead of my father David, but I am a little child; I do not know how to go out or come in. And your servant is in the midst of your people whom You have chosen, a great people, too numerous to be numbered or counted. "Therefore give to Your servant an understanding heart to judge Your people, that I may discern between good and evil. For who is able to judge this great people of yours?" The speech pleased the Lord, that Solomon had asked this thing. Then God said to him: Because you have asked this thing,

> and have not asked long life for yourself,
> nor have asked the life of your enemies,
> but have asked for yourself a wise and
> understanding heart, so that there has not
> been anyone like you before you, nor shall
> any like you arise after you. "And I have
> also given you what you have not asked:
> both riches and honor, so that there shall
> not be anyone like you among the kings
> all your days. "So if you walk in my ways,
> to keep my commandments, as your father
> David walked, then I will lengthen your
> days."

Now soon after God allowed a situation to test the wisdom He had given to Solomon. 1 Kings 3:16-28 states:

> Now two women who were harlots came
> to the king, and stood before him. And
> one woman said, "O my lord, this woman
> and I dwell in the same house; and I gave
> birth while she was in the house. "Then it
> happened, the third day after I had given
> birth, that this woman also gave birth.
> And we were together; no one was with
> us in the house, except the two of us in
> the house. "And this woman's son died
> in the night, because she lay on him. "So
> she arose in the middle of the night and
> took my son from my side, while your
> maidservant slept, and laid her dead child
> in my bosom. "And when I rose in the

morning to nurse my son, there he was, dead. But when I had examined him in the morning, indeed, he was not my son whom I had borne." Then the other woman said, "No! But the living one is my son, and the dead one is your son, and the living one is my son." Thus they spoke before the king. And the king said, "The one says, 'This is my son, who lives, and your son is the dead one; and the other says, 'No! But your son is the dead one, and my son is the living one.'" Then the king said, "Bring me a sword." So they brought a sword before the king. And the king said, "Divide the living child in two, and give half to one, and half to one, and half to the other." Then the woman whose son was living spoke to the king, for she yearned with compassion for her son; and she said, "O lord, give her the living child, and by no means kill him!" But the other said, "Let him be neither mine nor yours, but divide him." So the king answered and said, "Give the first woman the living child, and by no means kill him; she is the mother." And all Israel heard of the judgment which the king had rendered; and they feared the king, for they saw that the wisdom of God was in him to administer justice.

God blessed Solomon with so much wisdom that he was not only the wisest king, but the wisest man on earth. 1 Kings 4:29-34 says:

> And God gave Solomon wisdom and exceedingly great understanding, and largeness of heart like the sand on the seashore. Thus Solomon's wisdom excelled the wisdom of all men of the East and all the wisdom of Egypt. For he was wiser that all men-than Ethan the Ezrahite, and Heman, Chalcol, and Darda, the sons of Mahol; and his fame was in all the surrounding nations. He spoke three thousands proverbs, and his songs were one thousand and five. Also he spoke of trees, from the cedar tree Lebanon even to the hyssop that springs out of the wall; he spoke also of animals, of birds, of creeping things, and of fish. And men of all nations, from all the kings of the earth who had heard of his wisdom, came to hear the wisdom of Solomon.

As a benefit of God's wisdom working in his life, many would come to hear his wisdom and would bring offerings unto him. 1 Kings 10:1-10 we see this from the queen of Sheba:

> Now when the queen of Sheba heard of the fame of Solomon concerning the name of the lord, she came to test him with hard questions. She came to Jerusalem with a very great retinue, with camels that bore spices, very much gold, and precious stones; and when she came to Solomon, she spoke with him about all that was

in heart. So Solomon answered all her questions; there was nothing so difficult for the king that he could not explain to her. And when the queen of Sheba had seen all the wisdom of Solomon, the house that he had built, the food on his table, the seating of his servants, the service of his waiters and their apparel, his cupbearers, and his entryway by which he went up to the house of the Lord, there was no more spirit in her. Then she said to the king: "It was a true report which I heard in my own land about your words and your wisdom. However I did not believe the words until I came and saw with my own eyes; and indeed the half was not told me. Your wisdom and prosperity exceed the fame of which I heard. Happy are your men and happy are these servants, who stand continually before you and hear your wisdom! Blessed be the Lord your God, who delighted in you, setting you on the throne of Israel! Because the Lord has loved Israel forever, therefore He made you king, to do justice and righteousness." Then she gave the king one hundred and twenty talents of gold, spices in great quantity, and precious stones.

1 Kings 10:23-25 adds: So King Solomon surpassed all the kings of the earth in riches and wisdom. Now all the earth sought the presence of Solomon to hear his wisdom which God had put in his

heart. Each man brought his present: articles of silver and gold, garments, armor, spices, horses, and mules, at a set rate year by year.

GODLY WISDOM IN JOSEPH

The wisdom of God was also present in Joseph's life which brought him from the prison to Pharaoh's palace. Genesis 41:25-44:

> Then Joseph said to Pharaoh, "The dreams of Pharaoh are one; God has shown Pharaoh what He is about to do: "The seven good cows are seven years, and the seven good heads are seven; the dreams are one. "And the seven thin and ugly cows which came up after them are seven years, and the seven empty heads blighted by the east wind are seven years of famine. "This is the thing which I have spoken to Pharaoh. God has shown Pharaoh what he is about to do. "Indeed seven years of great plenty will come throughout all the land of Egypt; "but after them seven years of famine will arise, and all the plenty will be forgotten in the land of Egypt; and the famine will deplete the land. So the plenty will not be known in the land because of the famine following, for it will be very severe. And the dream repeated to Pharaoh twice because the thing is established by God, and God will shortly bring it to pass. "Now therefore,

let Pharaoh do this, and let him appoint officers over land, to collect one-fifth of the produce of the land of Egypt in the seven plentiful years. And let them gather all the food of those good years that are coming, and store up grain under the authority of Pharaoh, and let them keep food in the cities. Then that food shall be as a reserve for the land of Egypt, that the land may not perish during the famine." So the advice was good in the eyes of Pharaoh and in the eyes of all his servants. And Pharaoh said to his servants, "can we find such a one as this, a man in whom is the Spirit of God?" Then Pharaoh said to Joseph, "Inasmuch as God has shown you all this, there is no one as discerning and wise as you. You shall be over my house, and all my people shall be ruled according to your word; only in regard to the throne will I be greater than you." And Pharaoh said to Joseph, "See, I have set you over all the land of Egypt." Then Pharaoh took his signet ring off his hand and put it on Joseph's hand; and he clothed him in garments of fine linen and put a gold chain around his neck. And he had him ride in the second chariot which he had; and they cried before him, "Bow the Knee!" So he set him over the land of Egypt. Pharaoh also said to Joseph, "I am Pharaoh, and without your consent no man shall lift hand or foot in all the land of Egypt."

The Holy Spirit blessed Joseph to interpret the dreams and gave him the wisdom to save his people and the people of Egypt through a time of famine, thus exalting him to be governor over Egypt.

A PERSONAL ENCOUNTER

I had recently received the baptism of the Holy Ghost and He was using me more powerfully than ever before. One Tuesday night at prayer service, my pastor relayed a prayer request from a young woman. Her husband was in the military at that time and they were having marital problems. Her husband wanted a divorce though she was desperately trying to save their marriage. The pastor instructed us all to hold hands and pray. When it was my turn to pray, I could not seem to get my words together. It was as if I did not know how or what to pray. Suddenly, Romans 8:26-27 rose up in my spirit and I began to speak in tongues. One week later my pastor came back with a praise report regarding the young wife for which we had prayed. She called us "miracle workers" because her husband had a complete turnaround and instead of getting a divorce, they reconciled their marriage.

CHAPTER 3

Spirit of Understanding: Access Granted

Adam was made in God's image and likeness, however, he sinned. As a result of his sin the human race was brought under a curse of eternal damnation and separation from God. Therefore, in order to redeem man, God sent His only begotten Son to die as a Lamb sacrifice for the human race. Not only did Jesus come as our Savior, but he came to know us more intimately. Hebrews 4:15 says: *For we do not have a High Priest who cannot sympathize with our weakness, but was in all points tempted as we are, yet without sin.* The Spirit of understanding was upon Him to know and feel what man was dealing with physically, mentally and emotionally. Jesus was ridiculed, doubted, neglected, abandoned, sorrowful, cried, beaten, chastised, and forsaken. I believe that makes Jesus our greatest intercessor, because He knows what we are going through, because of what He went through Himself.

Understanding is defined as the act of one who understands. It is also the power or ability to learn and know; intellect; intelligence. Now this understanding, which comes from the Holy Spirit, will also allow our finite mind to comprehend and derive the plans and purposes of God. Proverbs 9:10 states: And the knowledge of the Holy One understands. 1 Corinthians 2:13-16 says: These things we also speak, not in words which man's wisdom teaches, but which the Holy Spirit teaches, comparing spiritual things with spiritual. But the natural man does not receive the things of the Spirit of God, for they are foolishness to him; nor can he know them, because they are spiritually discerned. But he who is spiritual judges all things, yet he himself is rightly judged by no one. For "who has known the mind of the Lord that he may instruct Him?" But we have the mind of Christ. The mind of Christ is the word of God. Jesus was filled with the Holy Spirit and was able to comprehend the things of God. Luke 2:40, 46-47: And the child grew and became strong in spirit, filled with wisdom; and the grace of God was upon him. Now so it was after three days they found him in the temple, sitting in the midst of the teachers, both listening to them and asking them questions. And all who heard Him were astonished at His understanding and answers. Even as an adolescent, the Holy Spirit was giving Him extraordinary intellect. At twelve years old, He understood the teachers and asked articulate questions to continue to gain more knowledge.

UNDERSTANDING AS A KEEPER

Understanding is a keeper also. Proverbs 2:11-12 tells us that: Understanding will keep you, To deliver you from the way of evil, from the man who speaks perverse things. Understanding God's word is very important. Failure to understand God's word will allow the devil will to steal it from you. Matthew 13:19: "When anyone hears the word of the kingdom, and does not understand it, then the wicked one comes and snatches away what was sown in heart. This is he who received seed by the wayside. John 10:10 says: The thief comes to steal, kill, and destroy. The devil wants to steal the word of God sown in your heart before you are able to produce a harvest in your life. He does not care if you come to church, sing in the choir, or shout and dance in the service. He is only afraid of those that hear and understand and apply it to their everyday lives.

UNDERSTANDING AND WISDOM

Now wisdom can also be defined as the application of understanding. That is why we see in the book of Proverbs the two being mentioned in the same scripture. Proverbs 4: 4-5 says: He also taught me, and said to me: "Let your heart retain my words; Keep my commands, and live. Get wisdom! Get understanding . . . ! Proverbs 1: 5-6 states: . . . And a man of understanding will attain wise counsel, To understand a proverb and an enigma, The words of the wise and their riddles. Jesus always spoke to the people in parables, but always explained them to the disciples so that they received the hidden message. Matthew 13:10-13 says: *And the disciples came and said to Him, "Why do you to them in parables?" He answered and said to them, "Because it has been given to you to know the mysteries of the kingdom of heaven, but to them it has not been given, "For whoever has, to him more will be given and he will have abundance; but whoever does not have, even what he has will be taken away from him. Therefore I speak to them in parables, because seeing they do not see, and hearing they do not hear, nor do they understand.* Jesus wants and needs us as Christian people to understand Him and His word so that He, by His Spirit, can bring forth manifestation in our lives. In Matthew 13:15 He says: *For the hearts of this people have grown dull. They are hard of hearing, and their eyes they have closed, lest they should see with their eyes and hear with their ears, lest they should understand with their hearts and turn, so that I should heal them.* That explains why the Holy Spirit is needed regarding the word of God. He will reveal a deeper comprehension of God's word so that we can receive it's benefits in our Christian walk.

UNDERSTANDING AS A GATEWAY

As I was preparing to write about the Spirit of Understanding, I was having trouble explaining this or even understanding this myself. One night as I was preparing to write about this topic, I asked the Lord what the Spirit of Understanding was? In response I heard the word "gateway." So I looked in Webster's dictionary and saw that the definition for "gateway" is a way in or out. Jesus said in John 10:9: *"I am the door, If anyone enters by me, he will be saved, and will go in and out and find pasture.* He also says in John 14:6: *"I am the way, the truth and the life. No one comes to the Father except through Me. Jesus is the "gateway" into all things and by the aid of the Holy Spirit we will be able to access more of our Savior and Redeemer.* Haleleujah!

MORE SCRIPTURES REGARDING UNDERSTANDING

2 Corinthians 1:20-22: For all the promises of God in Him are yes, and in Him Amen, to the glory of God through us. Now He who establishes us with you in Christ and has anointed us in God, who also has sealed us and given us the Spirit in our hearts as guarantee.

Ephesians 1:11-14: In Him also we have obtained an inheritance, being predestined according to the purpose of Him who works all things according to the counsel of His will, that we who first trusted in Christ should be to the praise of His Glory. In Him you also trusted, after you heard the word of truth, the gospel of your salvation; in whom also, having believed, you were sealed with the Holy of Promise, who is guarantee of our inheritance until the redemption of the purchased possession, to the praise of His glory.

Ephesians 1:17-19: that the God of our Lord Jesus Christ, the Father of glory, may give to you the spirit of wisdom and revelation in the knowledge of Him, the eyes of your understanding being enlightened; that you may know what is the hope of His calling, what are the riches of the glory of His inheritance in the saints, and what is the exceeding greatness of His power toward us who believe, according to the working of His mighty power.

Col. 1:9-17,19: For this reason we also, since the day we heard it, do not cease to pray for you, and to ask that you may be filled with the knowledge of His will in all wisdom and spiritual understanding; that you may worthy of the Lord, fully pleasing Him, being fruitful in every good work and increasing in the knowledge of God; strengthened with all might, according to His glorious power, for all patience and longsuffering with joy; giving thanks to the Father who has qualified us to be partakers of the inheritance of the saints in the light. He has delivered us from the darkness and conveyed us into the kingdom of the Son of His love, in whom we have redemption through His blood, the forgiveness of sins. He is the image of the invisible God, the firstborn over all creation. For by Him all things were created. For by Him all things were created that that are on earth, visible and invisible, whether thrones or dominions or principalities or powers. All things were created through Him and for Him. And he is before all things, and in Him all things consist. For it pleased the Father that in Him all the fullness should dwell.

CHAPTER 4

———⊗⊗⊗———

Spirit of Counsel: Guiding Light

What a wonderful Counselor that we have in the Holy Spirit. This allows Him to supernaturally administer counsel or advice to whomever He has chosen to receive this guidance. Counselor is one of the names given unto Jesus. Isaiah 9:6 says: *And His name will be called Wonderful, Counselor, Mighty God.*

Jesus advised, introduced and instructed the twelve apostles, whom His Father had chosen, about the ways of the Kingdom of God. In Matthew 6:33 Jesus says: *But seek ye first the kingdom of God and His righteousness and all these things will be added unto you.* At this very moment Jesus is sitting at the right hand of the Father. So, who then is going to continue to instruct us in the ways of the kingdom of God? The answer is the Holy Spirit. John 16:12-13 says: *"I still have many things to say to you, but you cannot bear them now. However, when He, the Spirit of truth, has come, He will guide you into all truth; for He will not speak on His own authority, but whatever He hears He will speak; and He will tell you things to come.* John 14:25-26 states: *"These things I have spoken to you while being present with you. "But the Helper, the Holy Spirit, whom the Father will send in My name, He will teach you all things, and bring to your remembrance all things that I said to you.* 1 John 2:27 says: *"But the anointing which you have received from Him abides in you, and you do not need that anyone teach you; but as the same anointing teaches you concerning all things, and is true, and is not a lie, and just as it has taught you, you will abide in Him.* The Holy Spirit will not only grant access to Jesus, but will also teach and advise us in the things that He has said. He will teach us about spiritual things. 1 Corinthians 2:13: *These we also speak, not in words which man's wisdom teaches, comparing spiritual things with spiritual.* By connection and fellowship through the Holy Spirit, He will lead us in our everyday lives. Romans 8:14 says: *For as many are led by the Spirit of God, these are the sons of God.* Another benefit to following the direction of the Holy Spirit is Life. Romans 8:1-8 says:

> There is therefore now no condemnation to those who are in Christ Jesus, who do not walk according to the flesh, according to the Spirit. For the law of the Spirit of

Life in Christ Jesus has made me free from the law of sin and death. For what the law could not do in that the law could not do in that it was weak through the flesh, God did by sending His own Son in the likeness of sinful flesh, on account of sin: He condemned sin in the flesh, that the righteous requirement of the law might be fulfilled in us who do not walk according to the flesh but according to the Spirit. For those who live according to the flesh set their mind on the things of the flesh, but those who live according to the Spirit, the things of the Spirit. For to be carnally minded is death, but to be spiritually minded is life and peace. Because the carnal mind is enmity against God; for it is not subject to the law of God, nor indeed can be. So then, those who are in the flesh cannot please God.

Now if we walk in the Spirit and heed His direction we will have the life that was given unto Adam. We will start to produce the fruits of the Spirit and not fulfill the lusts of the flesh. Galatians 5:17-25 states:

For the flesh lusts against the Spirit, and the Spirit against the flesh; and these are contrary to one another, so that you do not do the things that you wish. But if you are led by the Spirit, you are not under the law. Now the works of the flesh are evident, which are: adultery, fornication, uncleanness, lewdness. Idolatry, sorcery, hatred, contentions, jealousies, outbursts of wrath, selfish ambitions, dissensions, heresies, envy, murders, drunkenness, revelries, and the like; of which I tell you beforehand, just as I also told you in time past, that those who practice such things will not inherit the kingdom of God. But the fruit of the Spirit is love, joy peace, longsuffering, kindness, goodness, faithfulness, gentleness, self-control. Against such there is no law. And those who are Christ's have crucified the flesh with its passions and desires. If we live in the Spirit, let us also walk in the Spirit.

Walking in the Spirit produces rest for our mind, body and soul. When we accept Jesus Christ as our Lord and Savior, then our spirits are transformed and we become children of God. We are only called sons of God as we follow and are obedient to His words.

A PERSONAL ENCOUNTER

A young lady that I know confided in me about her ex-boyfriend. After she had given her life to Jesus, she could clearly see that he was no good for her. Yet and still, she would stumble in her flesh and end up sleeping with him. Though she tried to resist him, he would draw her in by making her laugh. I told her that I would pray that the next time that he tried to use humor to seduce her that she would not be moved and that she would be able to sever the relationship. Now, at the time, I assumed it was me speaking, when, in fact, it was the Holy Ghost speaking through me. The Holy Spirit moved very fast, because the next day she came and told me that everything that I said had come to pass. The ex-boyfriend came by the previous night with his comedy act in an attempt to make her smile and laugh. She told him that it had no effect on her and he got upset and left. God broke that "soul tie" so that she could be free to pursue the things of God.

CHAPTER 5

⸺ ◦◦◦ ⸺

The Spirit of Might Holy Ghost Strength

The Holy Spirit is very powerful and is full of rich resources. This can be categorized as the Spirit of Might. This might, derived from the Spirit of Grace, enables us to access a strength that will empower us to fulfill every assignment given by our Lord Jesus Christ. One Webster's definition of might is: *power* or *resources*. Now lets go deeper and find the definition of *power*: 1. Position of authority 2. Ability to act 3. One that has power 4. Physical might 5. Force or energy used to do work. The definition of *resource* is: 1: a new or reserve source 2. available funds 3. ability to handle situations.

Adam demonstrated the first definition of power in Genesis 1:26: Then God said, *"Let us make man in*

Our image, according to Our likeness; let them have dominion over the fish of the sea, over the birds of the air, and over the cattle, over every creeping thing that creeps on the earth." Adam was placed in the garden of Eden with full dominion and power over the full earth. He was given stewardship over the entire earth and was given the assignment of reproducing the image and likeness of God on the earth. Adam sinned and transgressed against God and he lost everything God gave him. He lost his power and authority plus fellowship with God and the Holy Spirit.

The might of the Holy Spirit is unlimited and knows no bounds. Zechariah 4:6 says: "So he answered to Zerubbabel: *Not by might nor by power, but by My Spirit,' Says the Lord of hosts.* The Holy Spirit is much greater than our might or power, because true might and power derive from the Spirit. That is why it is called the Spirit of might because this might comes only by the Spirit.

The Spirit of Might with Samson

The Spirit of might was also seen in Samson's life. He was ordained to be a judge over Israel and was to deliver the people from the hand of the Phillistines. The Spirit of the Lord would come upon him with great strength. Judges 14:5-6: *So Samson went down to Timnah with his father and mother, and came to the vineyards of Timnah. Now to his surprise, a young lion came roaring against him. And the Spirit of the Lord came mightily upon him, and he tore the lion apart as one would have torn apart a young goat, though he had nothing in his hand.* The Spirit of the Lord would come upon this man giving him superhuman strength and fighting ability to fight the Phillistines. Judges 15:14-15 adds: *When he came to Lehi, the Phillistines came shouting against him. Then the Spirit of the Lord came mightily upon him; and the ropes that were on his arms became like flax that is burned with fire, and his bonds broke loose from his hands. He found a fresh jawbone of a donkey, reached out his hand and took it, and killed a thousand men with it.*

THE SPIRIT OF MIGHT WITH DAVID

David was another prime example of one empowered by the Spirit of might. The Spirit of the Lord came upon him with boldness and faith as young boy and throughout his entire kingship.

In 1 Samuel 17:33-37, when the armies of Israel were facing Goliath, we can see the Spirit's might at work in young David:

> And Saul said, "You are not able to go against this Phillistine to fight with him for you are a youth, and he a man of war from his youth." But David said to Saul, "Your servant used to keep his fathers sheep, and when a lion or a bear came and took a lamb out of the flock, I went out after it and struck it, and delivered the lamb from its mouth; and when it arose

33

against me, I caught it by its beard and struck and killed it. Your servant has killed both lion and bear; and this uncircumcised Philistine will be like one of them, seeing he has defied the armies of the living God. Moreover David said, "The Lord who delivered me from the the paw of this bear, he will deliver me from the hand of the Phillistine." And Saul said to David, "Go and let the Lord be with you!"

David had confidence in the power of God and how He delivered his enemies into his hand. David had no fear of Goliath, because he was anointed by God to be a conqueror and a king. 1 Samuel 17:45-51 continues:

Then David said to the Phillistine, "You come to me with a sword, with a spear and a javelin. But I come to you in the name of the Lord of Hosts, the God of the armies of Israel whom you have defied. This day the Lord will deliver you into my hand, and I will strike you and take your head from you. And this day I will give the carcasses of the camp of the Philistines to the birds of the air and the wild beasts of the air and the wild beasts of the earth, that all the earth may know that there is a God in Israel. Then David put his hand in his bag and took out a stone; and he slung and struck the Philistine in his forehead, and fell on his face to earth. So David prevailed over the Philistines with a sling and a stone, and struck the Philistine and killed him. But there was no sword in the hand of David. Therefore David ran and stood over its sheath and killed him, and cut off his head with it. And when the Philistines saw that their champion was dead they fled.

David was also a prophet and even at a young age every thing that he told Goliath, God allowed it to come to pass. Another thing he did not use a sling shot, but the name of the Lord. That was his weapon of choice and after that the Phillistines knew about the God of Israel. I believe if David would have taken up any weapon, or maybe not used anything at all, he still would have come out with the victory. The Holy Spirit endorsed David by coming upon him; and by using only a sling shot and a rock, he killed Goliath. Not only was the Holy Spirit mighty through David, but also with his army. 2 Samuel 23:8-22 says:

These are the names of the men whom David had: Josheb-Bassheheth the Tachmonite, chief among the captains. He was called Adine the Eznite, because he had killed eight hundred men at one time. And after him Eleazar the son of Dodo, the Ahohite, one of the three mighty men with David when they the Phillistines who were gathered there for battle, and the men of Israel had retreated. He arose and attacked the Phillistines until his hand was weary and his hand was weary and his hand stuck to the sword. The Lord brought about a great victory that day; and the people retreated after him to plunder. And after him was Shammah the son of the Agee the Hararite. The Phillistines had gathered together into a troop where there was a piece of ground full of lentils. So the people fled from the Phillistines. But he stationed himself in the middle of the field defended it, and killed the Phillistines. So the Lord brought about a great victory. Then three of the thirty chief men went down at harvest time and came to David at the cave of Adullam. And the troop of Phillistines encamped in the Valley of Rephaim. David was in the stronghold, and the garrison of the Phillistines was then in Bethlehem, which is by the gate. So the three mighty men broke through the camp of the Phillistines, drew water from the well of Bethlehem that was by the gate, and took it to David. Nevertheless he would not drink, but poured it out to the Lord. And he said, "Far be it from me, O Lord, that I should do this! Is this not the blood of the men who went in jeopardy of their lives?" Therefore he would not drink it. These things were done by the three mighty men. Now Abishai, the brother of Joab, the son of Zeruiah, was chief of another three. He lifted his spear against three hundred men, killed them and won a name among these three. Was he not the most honored of the three? Therefore he became their captain. However, he did not attain to the first three. Benaiah was the son of Jehoiada, the son of a valiant man from Kabzeel, who had done many deeds. He had killed two lion-like heroes of Moab. He also had gone down and killed a lion in the midst of a pit on a snowy day. And he killed an Egyptian, a spectacular man. The Egyptian had a spear in his hand; so he went down to him with a staff, wrested the spear out of the Egyptian's hand, and killed him with his own spear. These things Benaiah the son of Jehoiada did, and won a name among three mighty men.

Also, the spirit of might will bless with endurance to run the race with patience and faith as we encounter trials and tribulations for the word's sake. Paul prays for the Ephesians. Ephesians 3:13-17:

Therefore I ask that you do not lose heart at my tribulations for you, which is your glory. For the reason I bow my knees to the Father of our Lord Jesus Christ. From whom the whole family in heaven and earth is named, that He would grant you, according to the riches of His glory, to be strengthened with might through His Spirit in the inner man that Christ may dwell in your hearts through faith.

Our inner man or spirit man is the only thing that has transformed and is like God. Jesus has redeemed our spirit man, but our flesh and mind are not. This is where we fall short everyday. We cannot sin in our spirit man, because it is born again and has the divine nature of God. The spirit of might will help us daily to overcome sin. Romans 6:12-14 says: *Therefore do not let sin reign in your mortal body, that you should obey in its lusts. And do not present your members of unrighteousness to sin but present yourselves to God as being alive from the dead and your members as instruments to God. For sin shall not have dominion over you, for you are not under law but under grace.* Jesus came and conquered sin, the sting of death, the grave, hell and the devil. He was able to take up the sins of the world because he knew no sin and therefore was mighty to overcome and conquer sin. Romans 12:1-2 says: *I beseech you therefore, brethren, by the mercies of God, that you present your body as a living sacrifice, holy, acceptable to God, which is your reasonable service. And do not be conformed to this world, but be ye transformed by the renewing of your mind that you may prove what is good and acceptable and perfect will of God.* Sin starts in the mind and if we think a thing then it will become a manifestation in our life. 2 Corinthians 10:4-6: *For the weapons of our warfare are not carnal but mighty in God for pulling down strongholds, casting down arguments and every high thing that exalts itself against the knowledge of God, bringing every thought into captivity to the obedience of Christ, and being ready to punish all disobedience when your obedience is fulfilled.* By the Holy Spirit and the word of God we have access to

His supernatural strength. When we are weak, then He is strong.

Romans 12:9-10 states: *And He said to me, "My grace is sufficient for you, for My strength is made perfect in weakness." Therefore most gladly I will rather in my infirmities, in reproaches, in needs, in persecutions, in distresses, for Christ's sake. For when I am weak, then I am strong.*

Romans 13:2-4 says: I have told you before, and foretell as if I were present the second time, and now being absent I write to those who have sinned before, and to all the rest that if I come again I will not spare since you seek a proof of Christ speaking in me, who is not weak toward you, but mighty in you. For though He was crucified in weakness, yet He lives by the power of God. For we also are weak in Him, but we shall live with him by the power of God toward you. God the Father is holy and true, his son Jesus Christ came as a man and never sinned and His Holy Spirit is also called the Spirit of Holiness.

Romans 1:4: *and declared to be the Son of God with power according to the Spirit of Holiness, by the resurrection from the dead.*

That is why he says be ye holy as your father who is in heaven.

CHAPTER 6

—⊗⊗⊗—

The Spirit of Knowledge

REVELATION TO ELEVATION

My people are destroyed for the lack of knowledge. (Hosea 4:6)

Webster's definition of knowledge is the awareness of facts, truths, or principals. God is all powerful and all knowing. He made everything and knows everything about the universe that He created. This attribute of God is called "omniscience". It is the attribute by which God perfectly and eternally knows all things that are known—past, present and future. God knows how to best attain to his desired ends. With this divine knowledge flowing through us, we are able to access the mind of God to extract God's infinite knowledge. Colossians 2:2-3 states: *that their hearts may be encouraged, being knit together in love, and attaining to all riches of the full assurance of understanding, to the knowledge of the mystery of God, both of the Father and of Christ, in whom are hidden all the treasures of wisdom and knowledge.* So in interpret those scriptures correctly then knowledge proceeds from the Father and the Son and they are called treasures.

Proverbs 8:10 says: *Receive my instruction, and not silver, and knowledge rather than choice gold.* God knows where your prosperity will come from and pleasing Him gives us insight to receive His blessings. Isaiah 45:3 states: *I will give you the treasures of darkness and hidden riches of secret places, that you may know that I, the Lord, Who calls you by your name, am the God of Israel.*

God's knowledge also brings forth life. Philippians 3:9-10 says: *Do not lie to one another, since you have put off the old man with his deeds, and have put on the new man who is renewed in knowledge according to the image of Him who created him.* God is so awesome that He will let us know a thing before it happens to let us know that He's eternal. He has seen everything from the beginning of creation to eternity past. Isaiah 46:9-10 states:

> Remember the former things of old, For I
> am God, and there is no other; I am God,
> and there is none like Me, Declaring the
> end from the beginning, And from ancient

> times things that are not yet done, Saying,
> "My counsel shall stand, And I will do
> all My pleasure, calling a bird of prey
> from the east, The man who executes My
> counsel, from a far country. Indeed I have
> spoken it; I will also bring it to pass. I
> have purposed it; I will also do it.

God allows His knowledge to flow through his gifts, that is, when the Holy Spirit manifests himself. 1 Corinthians 12:7-8, 10-11:

> But the manifestation of the Spirit is given
> to each one the profit of all: for to one is
> given the word of wisdom through the
> Spirit, to another the word of knowledge
> through the same spirit. To another
> prophecy, to another discerning of spirits,
> to another different kinds of tongues, to
> another the interpretation of tongues. But
> one and the same Spirit works all these,
> distributing to each one individually as He
> wills.

The spiritual gift of the "word of knowledge" deals with what exists past or present. By this gift God reveals to His servant via the Holy Spirit something that now exists or did exist on the earth. It has to be something this person has neither seen nor heard.

God gave the prophet Samuel knowledge to instruct Saul when he was enquiring of his lost donkeys:

So they went up to the city. As they were coming into the city, there was Samuel, coming out toward them on his way up to the high place. Now the Lord had told Samuel in his ear the day before Saul came saying, "Tomorrow about this time I will send you a man from the land of Benjamin, and you shall anoint him commander over Israel, that he may save My people from the hand of the Philistines; for I have looked upon My people, because their cry has come to Me." So when Samuel saw Saul, the Lord said to him, "There he is, the man of whom I spoke to you. This one shall reign over My people." Then Saul drew near to Samuel in the gate, and said, "Please tell me where is the seer's house?" Samuel answered Saul and said, "I am the seer. Go up before me to the high place, for you shall eat with me today; and tomorrow I will tell you all that is in your heart. "But as for your donkeys that were lost three days ago, do not be anxious about them, for they have been found. And on whom is all the desire of Israel? Is it not on you and all your father's house?"(1 Samuel 9:14-20)

God not only revealed that Saul lost his donkeys and they were found, but that it was the desire of his fathers and the house of Israel.

The prophet Elisha knowing the king of Syria's plans. 2 Kings 6:8-18 says:

> Now the king of Syria was making war against Israel; and he consulted with his servants, saying, "My camp will be in such and such a place." And the man of God sent to the king of Israel, saying, 'Beware that you do not pass this place, for the Syrians are coming down there." Then the king of Israel sent someone to the place of which the man of God had told him. Thus he warned him, and he was watchful there, not just once or twice. Therefore the heart of the king of Syria was greatly troubled by this thing; and he called his servants and said to them, "Will you not show me which of us is for the king of Israel?" And one of his servants said, "None my lord, O king; but Elisha, the prophet who is in Israel, tells the king of Israel the words that you speak in your bedroom.' So he said, "Go and see where he is, that I may send and get him." And it was told him, saying, "Surely he is in Dothan." Therefore he sent horses and chariots and a great army there, and they came by night and surrounded the city. And when the servant of the man of God arose early and went out, there was an army, surrounding the city with horses and chariots. And his servant said to him, "Alas, my master! What shall we do?" So he answered, "Do not fear, for those who

> are with us are more than those who are
> with them." And Elisha prayed, and said,
> "Lord, I pray open his eyes that he may
> see." Then the Lord opened the eyes of the
> young man, and he saw. And behold, the
> mountain was full of horses and chariots of
> fire all around Elisha. So when the Syrians
> came down to him, Elisha prayed to the
> Lord, and said, "Strike this people, I pray,
> with blindness." And He struck them with
> blindness according to the word of Elisha.

Not only did the Lord give Elisha the location of
the Syrian army, but advanced knowledge of every
move they made. Through such spiritual knowledge
the man of God was believed to be able to see into
king's bedchambers. God gave him the gift of spiritual
discernment which also allowed his servant to see
into the spirit realm and to see an army of angels on
chariots of fire.

PETER AND THE WORD OF KNOWLEDGE

Peter confessed that Jesus is the Christ, the son of
God. John 16:13-17 says:

> When Jesus came into the region of
> Caesarea Philippi, He asked His disciples,
> saying, "Who do men say that I, the Son
> of Man, am?" So they said, "Some say
> John the Baptist, some Elijah, and others
> Jeremiah or one of the prophets." He said

45

> to them, "But who do you say that I am?"
> Simon Peter answered and said, "You are
> the Christ, the Son of the living God."
> Jesus answered and said to him, "Blessed
> are you, Simon Bar-Jonah, for flesh and
> blood has not revealed this to you, but My
> Father who is in heaven.

God revealed to Peter's spirit that Jesus was indeed the son of God.

A Personal Experience

God has also allowed me to flow in the "word of knowledge" and the "word of wisdom" by dream. I had a dream that I was working at my job and in the dream there was a young woman who was a member of my church. We were working together and in the dream she told me that she does not like "fake" people. She said that she would rather people be themselves instead of trying to deceive her, because she can tell when someone is being authentic and when they only pretend to like her. The following Sunday I saw her at church and I told her the dream. She confirmed that everything that was revealed to me in the dream was true.

Another time, in October of 2010, my brother and I were on a cruise to Cozumel, Mexico. One Tuesday morning, as I slept in my cabin, I had a dream about my ex-wife. In the dream she was pregnant, but I perceived that I was not the father. Afterward, I awoke and could not get back to sleep. So I decided to get up and I walked around until I came to the front of the ship. We had just docked in Miridia and I began to pray to God. It was at that time when the Lord put it in my spirit to write this book and two others. Eventually, I went back to my room and saw that my brother had gone to eat breakfast. So I went back to sleep and I dreamed again about my ex-wife being pregnant. When I woke up, I found my brother and I told him about the dreams. My brother began to explain to me the significance of the two dreams, which were similar. He told me how Pharaoh had two dreams, (which were really one) and how Joseph explained to Pharaoh, by the Spirit of God, what Pharaoh dreamt twice. He showed him how these dreams would be established by God and would occur shortly thereafter.

A couple of months later, in January of 2011, I went to pick up my daughter and saw my ex-wife. As I was looking at her, I saw a little lump in her stomach. I started teasing her about her stomach and getting fat. I paused and thought about it and I asked her if she was pregnant. She hesitated, smiled, then answered "yes." I then knew for sure that God had allowed me to see something (in a dream) that was already present yet had no prior knowledge.

The Holy Spirit has shown and revealed things to me regarding Jesus and the word of God. Now I have heard that when one prays in the Spirit or in "tongues," that the devil does not understand what is being said. 1 Corinthians 2:7-8 states:

> *But we speak the wisdom of God in a mystery, the hidden wisdom which God ordained before the ages for our glory, which none of the rulers of this age knew, for had they known, they would not have crucified the Lord of Glory.*

1 Corinthians14:2 says:

> *For he who speaks in a tongue does not speak but to God, for no one understands him; however, in the spirit he speaks mysteries.*

JESUS AND THE WORD OF KNOWLEDGE

Now I know that Paul prayed in tongues, but I never heard of Jesus praying in the Spirit until now. In John, the eleventh chapter, the Holy Spirit showed me how Jesus was praying in the Spirit before he raised Lazarus from the dead. Jesus loved Lazarus and his sisters, Martha and Mary. Jesus knew that Lazarus was dead before He got to Bethany.

John 11: 11,13-14 says:

> *These things He said, and after that He said to them, "Our friend Lazarus sleeps, but I go that I may wake him up." However, Jesus spoke of his death, but they thought that He was speaking about*

> *taking rest in sleep. Then Jesus said to*
> *them plainly, "Lazarus is dead."*

We begin to see the human side of Jesus, because as He enters the atmosphere of grief and weeping, it affects Him also. John 11:33 says: *Therefore, when Jesus was saw her weeping, and the Jews who came with her weeping, He groaned in the spirit and was troubled. And he said, "Where have you laid him?" They said to Him, "Lord, come and see." Jesus wept.*

As I was reading this passage, the word "groan" jumped out at me and I saw it again in the thirty-eighth verse:

> *Then Jesus, again groaning in Himself,*
> *came to the tomb. It was a cave, and a*
> *stone lay against it.* Then I remembered
> where I had seen the word "groaning"
> and I turned to Romans 8:26 where it
> says: *Likewise the Spirit also helps in our*
> *weakness. For we do not know what we*
> *should pray for as we ought, but the Spirit*
> *makes intercession for us with groanings*
> *which cannot be uttered.*

Not only was He praying for Lazarus at this point, but He was also praying for Himself; because the spirit of grief was in that place and was trying to come upon Him. John 11:41-45 says:

> Then they took away the stone from the
> place where the dead man was lying. And

> Jesus lifted His eyes and said, "Father I thank you that You have heard Me. "And I know that You always hear Me, but because of the people who are standing by I said this, that they may believe that you have sent Me." Now when He said these things, He cried with a loud voice, "Lazarus, come forth!" And he who had died came out bound hand and foot with grave-clothes, and his face was wrapped with a cloth. Jesus said to them, "Loose him, and let him go." Then many of the Jews who had come to Mary, and had seen the things Jesus did, believed in Him.

Jesus began to thank the Father for hearing His prayer on behalf of Lazarus, but we do not see Him pray for Lazarus at any time. He was, however, praying in the Holy Spirit and He knew that God had heard Him. (Also He could not tell the people to leave because of their unbelief as when He had raised Jairus' daughter from the dead.) They believed that Jesus could have healed Lazarus of his sickness, that is why Martha said, ". . . *If you had been here Lord, my brother would not have died* (John 11:21). They knew Jesus as a healer, but not as a worker of miracles.

A REVELATION OF PERFECT LOVE

I was curious about John 7:38; where Jesus says," . . . out of his belly shall flow rivers of living water." In the next verse it is revealed that this "living water" is the Holy Spirit. I thought to myself, "What does this living water mean?" So one day, while working, the Lord impressed on my heart 1 John 4:18, which says: *There is no fear in love; but perfect love cast out fear, because fear involves torment. But he who fears has not been made perfect in love.*

Now as God was continuing to magnify that "perfect love casts out fear," 1 John 4:8 came to my mind which says ". . . God is love."* Afterwards He showed me 2 Timothy 1:7: *For God has not given us a spirit of fear, but of power and of love and a sound mind.* He followed with Acts 1:8: *But you shall receive power when the Holy Spirit has come upon you . . .* Finally, the last scripture that came to mind was Matthew 12:28 *"But if I cast out demons by the Spirit of God . . ."* That is when the "light" came on and I understood that this "perfect love" is referring to the Holy Spirit.

God the Father, God the Son, and God the Holy Ghost are One and They are Love. The Father and the Son are seated in Heaven; so the only God who dwells with us is the Holy Spirit. As we are led by the Holy Spirit as Jesus was, He will enable us to walk in His power and by His agape love to minister to His people who are in bondage to the enemy. Romans 5:5 says: *Now hope does not disappoint, because the love of God has been poured out in our hearts by the Holy Spirit who was given to us.* He also revealed to me that as our mind is transformed, by the word of God to love Him and His people, that the manifestation of

51

His presence will come and His gifts will flow in our lives. That is why 1 Corinthians 13:1-3 chapter was all about love, because it says if you do not have love it "profits you nothing."

Though I speak with the tongues of men and of angels, but have not love, I have become sounding brass or a clanging cymbal. And though I have the gift of prophecy, and understand all mysteries and all knowledge, and though have all faith, so that I could remove mountains, but have not love, I am nothing. And though I bestow all my goods to feed the poor, and though I give my body to be burned, but have not love, it profits me nothing.

It is love that activates everything in our lives, because that is the embodiment of God Himself. He loves us, that is why He gave up His Son.

CHAPTER 7

---∞∞∞---

The Spirit of the Fear of the Lord

Mighty is the Lord and great is His power. He overshadows us with His presence and His love is everlasting. His grace and mercy abounds to great heights and His blood washes away sin which gives us access through the veil until the Holiest of All. I thank you for want you have done and I love because who you are.

The word "fear" in the English language has two meanings: (1)unpleasant emotion caused by expectation or awareness of danger; to be afraid and (2) awe and reverence that a person of sense feels in the presence of God and, to a lesser extent, in the presence of a king or other dread authority.

Psalms 33:18-19: *Behold, the eye of the Lord is on those who fear Him, On those who hope in His mercy, To deliver their soul from death, And to keep them alive in famine.* Psalms 34:7,9: *The angel of the Lord encamps all around those who fear Him, and delivers them. Oh, fear the Lord, you His saints! There is no want to those who fear him.* Psalms 85:8-9: *I will hear what God the Lord will speak, For he will speak peace To His people and to His saints; But let them not turn back to folly. Surely His salvation is near to those who fear Him, That glory may dwell in our land.* Psalms 111:5 *He has given food to those who fear him; He will ever be mindful of His covenant.* Psalms 128:1-4: *Blessed is every one who fears the Lord, Who walk in His ways. When you eat the labor of your hands, You shall be happy, and it shall be well with you. Your wife shall be like a fruitful vine In the very heart of your house, Your children like olive plants all around you're your table. Behold, thus shall the man be blessed Who fears the Lord.* Proverbs 22:4: *By humility and the fear of the Lord are riches and honor and life.* Malachi 4:2: *But to you who fear My name The Sun of Righteousness shall arise With healing in His wings; And you shall go out And grow fat like stall-fed calves.* Acts 10:34-35: *In truth Peter opened his mouth and said: "In truth I perceive that God shows no partiality. But in every nation whoever fears Him and works righteousness is accepted by Him.*

Abraham and the Fear of the Lord

One of the first instances where we see God manifesting the Fear of the Lord in a believer's life is with Abraham. God appeared to him and told him to get away from his people and his country and follow Him. He told Abraham that he would make him a great nation, make his name great, make him a blessing, and all of his families would be blessed. We read throughout Genesis how God brought everything that He promised Abraham to pass and blessed him with a son. Years later, God tested Abraham by asking him to sacrifice his only son Isaac. Genesis 22:1-2 states: *Now it came to pass after these things that God tested Abraham, and said to him, "Abraham!" And he said, "Here I am." Then He said, "Take now your son, your only son, your only son Isaac, whom you love, and go to the land of Moriah, and offer him there as a burnt offering on one of the mountains of which I shall tell you."* Abraham had so much faith and honor for God that he believed that if God took his son, then He would have to provide him with another one; since He promised that He would give him a son. In the act of obedience to the Lord, God stopped Abraham from sacrificing Isaac and gave him yet another blessing for fearing Him:

> Genesis 22:9-13, 15-18: Then they came to the place of which God had told him. And Abraham built an altar there and placed the wood in order; and he bound Isaac his son and laid him on the altar, upon the wood. And Abraham stretched out his hand and

took the knife to slay his son. But the Angel of the Lord called to him from heaven and said, "Abraham, Abraham!" So he said, "Here I am." And he said, "Do not lay your hand on the lad, or do anything to him; for now I know that you fear God, since you have not withheld your son, your only son, from Me." Then Abraham lifted his eyes and looked, and there behind him was a ram caught in a thicket by its horns. So Abraham went and took the ram, and offered it up for a burnt offering instead of his son. Then the Angel of the Lord called to Abraham a second time out of heaven, and said: "By Myself I have sworn, says the Lord, because you have done this thing, and have not withheld your son, your only son-" blessing I will bless you, and multiplying I will multiply your descendants as the stars of the heaven and as the sand which is on the seashore; and your descendants shall possess the gate of their enemies. "In your seed all the nations of the earth shall be blessed, because you have obeyed My voice.

THE FEAR OF ISAAC

Isaac, Abraham's son, also benefitted from flowing in the Fear of the Lord, when sowing in a famine land. Genesis 26:1-6 says:

There was a famine in the land, besides the first famine that was in the days of Abraham. And Isaac went to Abimelech king of the Phillistines, in Gerar. Then the Lord appeared to him and said: Do not go down to Egypt; live in the land of which I shall tell you. "Dwell in this land, and I will be with you and bless you; for to you and your descendants I will give all these lands, and I will perform the oath which I swore to Abraham your Father. "And I will make your descendants all these lands; and in your seed all the nations of the earth shall be blessed; because Abraham obeyed My voice and kept My charge, My commandments, My statues, and My Laws." So Isaac dwelt in Gerar.

Isaac wanted to go back to Egypt where his father was blessed by God through Pharaoh, but God wanted to bless him in a new way: in famine land! Now imagine staying where your finances are drying up and God tells you to stand still and that He will restore everything that you have lost. Its so amazing because I believe that as he obeyed, God gave him peace. In the same way, when you obey His divine instruction, a peace will come over you which passes all understanding. In that same year God performed His word and Isaac received a hundredfold and he continued to propser. Genesis 26:12-16 states: *Then Isaac sowed in that land, and reaped in the same year a hundredfold; and the Lord blessed. The man began to prosper, and continued prospering until he became very prosperous; for he had possessions of herds and a great number of servants. So the Phillistines envied him. Now the Phillistines had stopped up all wells which his father's servants had dug in the days of Abraham his father, and they had fiiled them with earth. And Abimelech said to Isaac, "Go away from us, for you are much mightier than we."* God not only fulfilled His word, but made him mightier than a king.

Noah and Fear of the Lord

Noah also feared God when building the ark. Hebrews 11:7 says: *By faith Noah, being divinely warned of things not yet seen, moved with godly fear, prepared an ark of the saving of his household, by which he condemned the world and became heir of the righteousness which is according to faith.* Noah and his family were the only people on earth whose seed was not corrupted with the race of giants that were on the earth at this time. Genesis 6:1-14,17-22:

> Now it came to pass when men began to multiply on the face of the earth, and daughters were born to them, daughters of men, that they were beautiful; and they took wives for themselves of all whom they chose. And the Lord said, "My Spirit shall not strive with man forever, for he is indeed flesh; yet his days shall be one hundred and twenty years." There were giants on the earth in those days, and also afterward, when the sons of God came

in to the daughters of men and they bore children to them. Those were the mighty men who were of old, men of renown. Then the Lord saw that the wickedness of man was great in the earth, and that every intent of the thoughts of his heart was only evil continually. And the Lord was sorry that He had made man on the earth, and He was grieved in His heart. So the Lord said, "I will destroy man whom I have created from the face of the earth, both man and beast, creeping thing and birds of the air, for I am sorry that I have made them." But Noah found grace in the eyes of the Lord. This the genealogy of Noah. Noah was a just man, perfect in his generations. Noah walked with God. And Noah begot three sons: Shem, Ham, and Japeth. The earth also was corrupt before God, and the earth was filled with violence. So God looked upon the earth, and indeed it was corrupt; for all flesh had corrupted their way on earth. And God said to Noah, "The end of all flesh has come before Me, for the earth is filled with violence through them; and behold, I will destroy them with the earth." Make yourself an ark of gopher wood; make rooms in the ark, and cover it inside and outside with pitch." And behold, I Myself am bringing flood waters on the earth, to destroy from under heaven all flesh in which is the breathe of life; everything that is on the earth shall die."

> But I will establish My covenant with you;
> and you shall go into the ark-you, your
> sons, your wife, and your sons' wives with
> you. "And of every living thing of all flesh
> you shall bring two of every sort into the
> ark, to keep them alive with you; they shall
> be male and female. "Of the birds after
> their kind will come to you to keep them
> alive. "And you shall take for yourself of
> all food that is eaten, and you shall gather
> it to yourself; and it shall be food for you
> and for them." Thus Noah did: according
> to all that God commanded him so he did.

I believe that the Fear of the Lord produces obedience, honor and love. In this relationship with the Holy Spirit He will tell you what will oftentimes seem like crazy things to do. However, if we show love by being obedient unto His instructions, then we will reap great and mighty things through our Lord and Savior Jesus Christ.